An Owl, That's Who!

Autumn Leigh

Rosen REAL READERS

Rosen Classroom Books & Materials™
New York

An owl is a bird.

An owl can fly.

An owl has sharp claws.

An owl has big eyes.

An owl has feathers.

Do you know what sound an owl makes?

Words to Know

claws

eyes

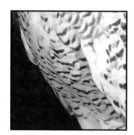

feathers

fly

owl